20 TELL-TALE SIGNS YOU'RE WITH A NARCISSISTIC LOVE BOMBER

20 TELL-TALE SIGNS YOU'RE WITH A NARCISSISTIC LOVE BOMBER

Get Out!

ALEXANDRIA O'NEAL

CONTENTS

Introduction

The initial encounter I had with the term "Love Bomb" transpired recently. At the time, I was immersed in crafting the fifth installment of my memoir series, entitled "Hallways of Her Past: A Timid Soul."

The writing process led me into the depths of introspection, prompting me to ponder on my mistakes, vulnerability and susceptibility during my past relationship with Maverick.

As I meticulously edited my series, I was compelled to confront and relive the episodes of my past, unearthing feelings of inferiority and frailty that dominated my existence in his presence.

Reflecting on those times brought forth a whirlwind of emotions, and I found myself ensnared by self-doubt, questioning my past decisions and berating myself for my perceived naivety. The shame of my past vulnerability was palpable, as I grappled with the resurgence of those debilitating emotions.

In today's digital age, discussions surrounding narcissism are pervasive across social media platforms. During a candid conversation with my friend Allison, about this very topic, she shared a TikTok video elucidating the concept of Love Bombing—a term unfamiliar to me until that moment.

My initial misconception led me to equate Love Bombing with narcissism. However, a deep dive into research revealed the stark distinction between the two, unraveling the reality that Maverick embodied the traits of a "Love-Bombing Narcissist."

This revelation was nothing short of an epiphany, exposing me to a complex phenomenon that potentially wreaks havoc on countless relationships and individuals, perhaps more than we could fathom.

Recognizing the relevance and connection to my memoir series, I felt a profound sense of responsibility to illuminate this issue, striving to raise awareness and shed light on a subject that had previously eluded my understanding, and possibly the consciousness of many others.

Twenty Unmistakable Signs You're Being Love Bombed

Number One
He totally overwhelms you with affection and adoration

From the very beginning, Alexi—whom you playfully nickname "Sexi Alexi" for his irresistible charm—plunges you into a world brimming with unadulterated adoration, overwhelming you with extravagant gifts and fervently whispering endless streams of heartfelt compliments.

You're swept up in a whirlwind of passion, where you find yourself the unequivocal center of his affections, enshrouded in his sincere and unwavering love. His lavish displays of affection and the perpetual outpouring of adoration weave an atmosphere of enchantment and romance, rendering every shared moment akin to the pages of an epic love story. His grandiose gestures and the relentless torrent of affection envelop you, crafting an ethereal realm of ardor and infatuation.

The intensity of his love is so commanding it feels as though you're lifted into the air, making you feel treasured and esteemed beyond your wildest dreams.

The consistent attention and dedication he bestows upon you paint your reality with the hues of a dreamlike romance—one that has taken a breathtaking turn from fantasy into captivating reality.

The way Alexi—your "Sexi Alexi"—lavishes

his love so freely and copiously imprints upon your heart, nurturing a bond that resonates with profound depth and an almost celestial connection.

His every action speaks volumes of his emotions, presenting a level of affection and care that is as extraordinary as it is deeply moving.

Around him, you bask in an aura of tenderness and warmth, assured in your worth and ceaselessly enveloped in love. The certainty of his devotion and the magnanimity of his love eradicate any lingering uncertainties, affirming his place in your life as someone truly remarkable.

The grandeur of his love, coupled with the

sensation of being adored within his universe, composes a romance that is both extraordinary and transcendental.

In the presence of Alexi's profound adoration and his capacity to revolutionize your existence with his love, you find yourself at the heart of a real-life love story—one that is as overwhelming as it is unforgettable, all through the grace of "Sexi Alexi's" profound affection.

Number Two
Non-Stop Notifications

The phenomenon of "Non-Stop Notifications" becomes deeply personal when you're caught in the whirlwind of Non-Stop Nancy's ardor.

Your phone transforms into a vessel of her affection, constantly alight with new messages, calls, and notifications that form a lifeline between you and her. Each buzz and ring is a digital heartbeat, a rhythm that now pulses through your daily life.

With Non-Stop Nancy, the space between real and virtual blurs, as the non-stop communication forges an intimacy that feels both exhilarating and intense.

Your phone, once just a tool, is now the canvas where your connection with Nancy gains color and texture, each notification painting another stroke on the masterpiece that is your relationship.

The messages from Nancy are like strings that tether your hearts together, her digital presence a constant whisper in your ear. To ignore your phone is to ignore the siren call of this connection, a connection so vivid and consuming that the rest of the world dims in comparison.

Each ping from Non-Stop Nancy is a pulse of something extraordinary, a rush of dopamine that cements the significance of what you're building together.

These are not just texts; they are the threads of a narrative you both are writing—a love story that unfolds in real-time, with every "ding" a confirmation of the unique dance you're sharing.

Being swept up in Non-Stop Nancy's tide means surrendering to a flow of communication that never ebbs.

It's a dance of digits across your phone screen, a symphony of soft electronic chimes that together compose the soundtrack of your burgeoning romance.

In the enchanting haze of Nancy's non-stop messaging, you find your reality punctuated by the light of her digital presence. Her commitment to this constant connection casts a glow on your everyday experiences, imbuing them with a sense of magic and boundless potential.

Non-Stop Nancy's vibrant energy, delivered through ceaseless digital interactions, wraps you in a narrative rich with promise and passion. It's a romance that doesn't pause for breath, a narrative where each notification is a vow, each call a serenade, and each day another chapter in a tale that promises to be nothing short of epic.

Number Three
Fast and Furious Romance

The tale titled "Fast and Furious Romance" captures the dizzying pace of your unfolding relationship with Fast Freddy—a tempo so breakneck and intense that it verges on the surreal.

With scarcely a moment to process, you find Fast Freddy not just entering your life, but sprinting through it, his presence filling your personal space with an immediacy that is as exhilarating as it is disconcerting.

It begins with the arrival of Fast Freddy's beloved couch at your doorstep—a gesture that treads a fine line between endearing and presumptuous. This isn't merely an act of relocating a cherished item; it's a calculated encroachment, a couch-sized Trojan horse ushering in a new era of your relationship. The unspoken messages are loud and clear: he's here to stay, ready or not.

As Fast Freddy's personal effects slowly infiltrate every corner of your abode, the once-clear boundaries of your solitude begin to fade. Your sanctuary is no longer just yours; it's becoming a testament to the fusion of lives, a tangible sign of the head-spinning velocity at which your partnership with Fast Freddy is progressing.

The pace at which this transformation occurs could rival the most viral dances lighting up

TikTok—fast, furious, and unrelenting. Your days and nights with Fast Freddy are a blur, where the lines between dating and living together are smudged beyond recognition.

While the dynamic energy of this rapid evolution is undeniably thrilling, it also tests your ability to adapt. There's barely a moment to catch your breath, to weigh the implications, or to truly question whether the path you're on with Fast Freddy is the one you envisioned for yourself.

Your romance with Fast Freddy is a testament to change and emotion, racing ahead with the force of a tempest.

It's a narrative of closeness and acceleration, mapping the trajectory of a relationship that rushes forward, leaving you exhilarated yet pondering if the pace is sustainable, if the rush is what you truly need.

Number Four
Dreaming Big, But It's Just Dreams

"Dreaming Big, But It's Just Dreams" brings to the forefront the enigmatic allure of Dreamy Darla, a master at crafting the most enticing visions of a future brimming with love, shared triumphs, and endless possibilities.

With her persuasive charm and unwavering confidence, she sketches out a tantalizing picture of what could be, inviting you into her tapestry of grand plans.

Each word from Dreamy Darla is like a stroke from a painter's brush, creating a vivid tableau of a future so appealing that you're swept up in the rhapsody of her dreams. She weaves her narrative with the finesse of a storyteller, making the life she describes appear within reach, and all the more alluring because of her infectious enthusiasm and the vividness of her vision.

Yet, as time progresses and you navigate through the layers of promises and pledges, the luster of Dreamy Darla's envisioned paradise begins to dim. Glimmers of reality pierce through the elaborate dreamscape, and questions arise about the feasibility of these glossy aspirations.

The dreams, once so vivid and engaging, show signs of fraying at the edges, gradually exposing their true nature as beautifully spun, yet fragile, fantasies.

The more you examine the fabric of Dreamy Darla's creations, the more apparent it becomes that they may be destined to remain as mere dreams—beautiful, but transient and ungrounded. The foundations of her promised world seem to be made of shifting sands, inspiring wonder, but lacking the substance needed to bring them into reality.

This dawning realization is unsettling, pitting the intoxicating beauty of Dreamy Darla's dreams against the stark truth of their intangibility.

You are left to wrestle with a dichotomy: the enchantment of the future she has painted and the sobering understanding that these vistas might forever be horizons that recede as you approach them.

Ultimately, "Dreaming Big, But It's Just Dreams" is a poignant musing on the importance of discerning heartfelt promises from hollow words.

It underscores the delicate line between the romantic allure of Dreamy Darla's persuasive narratives and the concrete actualization of those visions, drawing attention to the chasm that can exist between seductive assurances and their manifestation into reality.

Number Five
Sweet, Then Sour

Navigating the "Sweet, Then Sour" dynamic is like being strapped into an emotional rollercoaster, especially when you're dealing with someone like Sammy.

In his sweeter moments, he personifies affection, surrounding you with a romantic aura that leaves you feeling deeply cherished.

This version of him, Sweet Sammy, whispers love-filled promises and casts a spell of idealistic romance, offering a glimpse into a perfect world.

Yet, this delightful state is often as transient as a shooting star. A trivial trigger, like a pause to glance at a text message, can morph Sweet Sammy into his alter ego, Sour Sammy. It's as if the sunshine of his warm presence is eclipsed by a sudden frost. The shift is tangible; where there was once the comfort of his warmth, now the air bristles with a cold that creeps into the space between you.

You notice the stormy glint in Sour Sammy's eyes, clouded with suspicion, and his once sweet words now carry a bitter edge, laden with passive-aggressive barbs or thinly veiled critiques.

This jarring transformation leaves you disoriented, scrambling to understand how the tender moments could evaporate so swiftly.

Sweet Sammy's unpredictability sets you on a

perpetual tiptoe, wary of what might tilt the balance next. His whims dictate the emotional climate, and the constant oscillation between affection and indifference renders the atmosphere fraught with uncertainty.

You're left pondering the sincerity of the affection when Sweet Sammy is in his element. Were those moments of tenderness genuine, or merely a prelude to the next wave of chill from Sour Sammy? The sweetness, once pure and convincing, now carries a shadow of skepticism, and you find yourself analyzing every gesture for its true intent.

This "Sweet, Then Sour" pattern not only highlights the volatility of such relationships but also the inner turmoil they evoke.

The blend of affection with sudden disaffection creates a disconcerting rhythm, one where the highs are ecstatic but the lows leave you bracing for the next turn, unsure if you're about to encounter the delightful Sweet Sammy or weather the storm of Sour Sammy.

Number Six
Me, Myself, and I

"Me, Myself, and I" aptly characterizes a type of interaction dominated by one individual's narratives, where conversations invariably orbit around their life, triumphs, and ongoing sagas.

When engaging with Me-Me Megan, it often feels like being an audience member at a one-person show, where she is the perennial headliner.

Me-Me Megan has an uncanny knack for steering any dialogue back to her universe, constantly ensuring she is the nucleus around which all discussion spins. She dives into tales of her victories, laments her obstacles, and relishes in the minutiae of her personal dramas, painting every conversation with the broad strokes of her experiences.

In this lopsided dialogue, the imbalance is stark. Me-Me Megan's voice drowns out others, leaving little room for anyone else's narrative. Your contributions are sidelined, often lost in the shadow of her commanding presence. As she animatedly spins her yarns, any hope for a genuine exchange dwindles under the weight of her one-sided discourse.

The essence of conversation is lost as Me-Me Megan unwittingly transforms the dialogue into her monologue, her stage. While she may bask in the limelight of her storytelling, the dynamic she creates often eclipses the possibility of a balanced, reciprocal exchange of ideas and stories.

Consequently, her conversational monopoly can engender a feeling of marginalization, as if your voice and experiences are merely footnotes in the grand autobiography of Me-Me Megan.

This pattern can breed frustration and the sentiment that your own stories, no less rich or compelling, remain untold and underappreciated in the persistent shadow of her soliloquies.

In essence, being caught in the "Me, Myself, and I" dynamic with Me-Me Megan is a lesson in patience and listening, as what could be a rich

tapestry of shared human experience becomes a
monochrome narrative, woven with a single
thread — hers.

Number Seven

Needs Ghosted: Connection Lost

Ghostin' Gary perfectly embodies the imbalance of a relationship devoid of emotional reciprocity. In this dynamic, attempts at finding empathy or support vanish into the void, highlighting the disconcerting invisibility within his emotional landscape.

In this skewed bond, it's like peering through a one-way mirror. You can see deep into Gary's world, but your own image—and therefore your needs—remain unseen.

When you reach out, seeking connection and understanding, it's as though your pleas go unheard, like whispers lost in the void, leaving you to grapple with the resounding silence.

You find yourself disproportionately carrying the weight of emotional labor, becoming the lone guardian of your inner world, steering through your emotions without guidance or acknowledgment.

Ghostin' Gary's neglect towards your emotional well-being sends a piercing message: your feelings are not even a blip on his radar.

This consistent negation of your emotional needs slowly chips away at the bedrock of your self-worth. Doubts creep in, quietly suggesting that perhaps your emotional landscape is too vast, too complex, to coexist with such a partner.

As this one-sided narrative unfolds, a gulf

opens, echoing with the sound of your needs that go unmet and the coldness of emotional isolation. The heartfelt connection that should bind two people is absent, leaving you to float in the vast silence of unshared feelings.

"Needs Ghosted: Connection Lost" serves as a poignant narrative of emotional neglect in a relationship, testament to how a lack of empathy and recognition can carve out the core of a union, casting one into solitude—not just alone, but invisible and unheard in the profound silence of their solitary emotional journey.

Number Eight
Guilt-Tripping Like a Pro

Establishing boundaries with someone like Guilt-Trip Gina can be an incredibly challenging experience. She has a remarkable talent for twisting situations to her advantage and manipulating feelings with finesse.

Interactions with her often lead to second-guessing your decisions and being suffused with guilt, as though you're the one at fault.

Ever the master of subtle sabotage, Gina undermines your attempts to set limits while crafting the image of herself as the perennial victim.

She wields a whole arsenal of tactics designed

to burden you with guilt and doubt, leading you to question whether your need for personal boundaries is unreasonable—or worse, selfish. Facing Guilt-Trip Gina can feel like facing a grandmaster in the art of emotional manipulation, someone who knows exactly how to pull the strings to her benefit.

Such relentless guilt-tripping can summon a torrent of negative emotions, leaving you feeling confused, frustrated, and utterly exhausted.

Your efforts to safeguard your personal space and uphold your well-being seem to be thwarted at every turn. There are moments when you might find yourself relenting, loosening your boundaries just to sidestep confrontation or the distressing sensation of being cast as the villain.

As time wears on, the continuous emotional manipulation can erode your sense of autonomy, leading to feelings of powerlessness in your own life narrative.

You're incessantly nudged, if not shoved, into prioritizing her needs and desires above your own. This toxic cycle not only impairs your ability to stand your ground but also fosters a lopsided relationship dynamic that is inherently unhealthy and unsustainable.

Number Nine
Drama on Repeat

In this unending cycle of 'Drama on Repeat', it feels as though your world has been flipped upside down, landing squarely in the middle of a reality TV show—minus any glitz or glam.

Instead of a star-studded spectacle, your days have turned into a never-ending rollercoaster of emotional highs and lows, with each new twist and turn orchestrated by Drama Drew, who seems to bring a surprise that fosters an atmosphere ripe with uncertainty and chaos.

Day in and day out, you're bombarded by relentless drama, with each new episode crafted by Drew seemingly more intense and conflict-laden than the last. He appears to be the director who thrives on the stress and emotional turmoil that's become your reality, leaving you drained as you navigate through the chaos he orchestrates.

Patterns begin to emerge, a narrative riddled with recurring themes of conflict and tension, mirroring the predictable arcs of reality TV dramas.

But in your life, these patterns are anything but entertaining—they're destructive and draining, slowly stripping away the joy and tranquility from your existence, with Drama Drew often at the epicenter, seemingly feeding off the disorder.

The constant upheaval makes it hard to find

stable ground, and you may begin to wonder what a peaceful, drama-free existence even resembles anymore. The ongoing tumult overshadows your serenity, as you find yourself perpetually on edge, bracing for the next upheaval.

Caught in the thick of this relentless drama, you might find yourself longing for an escape, aching for stability and the calm of a life untouched by this chaos.

It becomes clear that while you can turn off a reality TV show, stepping out of Drama Drew's live-action version is an entirely different challenge—one that is far less appealing.

Number Ten
Social Sleuth

The "Social Sleuth" takes on intriguing new layers with Snoopy Sophia, highlighting an individual whose interest in your life reaches new heights.

She's not satisfied with a mere glance at recent updates; instead, she dives into the depths of your social media history, resurfacing posts and photos that have long faded from your memory.

Her exploration surpasses what many would consider normal online interaction, revealing a level of curiosity that might be seen as overzealous.

Her interactions with long-buried images in your albums, leaving a trail of likes and comments, are testament to her thorough sweep through your digital legacy. Every corner of your online world, from old snapshots to forgotten festivities and casual throwbacks, falls under her keen scrutiny.

Initially, her engagement might seem like genuine interest, but the thoroughness of her search can come across as overstepping. She seems to have meticulously mapped every corner of your digital footprint, examining each post and picture with great attention to detail.

This behavior triggers mixed feelings. On one hand, it shows a commitment to really get to know you. On the other, it highlights a disregard for boundaries, prompting you to think more critically about your privacy online.

In the end, Snoopy Sophia's presence in your digital sphere goes from curious to potentially invasive, her eagerness to uncover your history leaving you with a complex blend of flattery and discomfort.

Number Eleven
Exes on Parade

"Exes on Parade" portrays a situation in which the individual you're engaging with, known among friends as Playboy Pete for his notable romantic history, often brings up his former relationships during conversations.

It seems he has a comprehensive roster of past partners and a rich tapestry of stories about them, ready to be woven into your dialogues. This isn't an occasional nostalgic trip; it's a habitual and almost systematic narration of past romances that's become a recurring theme when you interact.

He ensures that each tale serves dual

purposes: to highlight his extensive dating past and to underscore how you differ, ostensibly in a superior way. He narrates his experiences in a way that tends to paint his exes in an unflattering light, focusing on the shortcomings and mishaps of those relationships.

Through these stories, his agenda becomes apparent: he aims to impress upon you that he has never met anyone quite like you, casting you as the pinnacle of his romantic history.

Playboy Pete wants you to feel exceptionally special, as though you're the prize at the end of a long and arduous dating quest. While this may at first seem complimentary, a closer look might reveal red flags.

The frequent mentions of past flames, a habitual tactic of his, can become tiresome and impose an unwanted dynamic in your budding relationship, prompting questions about his fixation on the past and his compulsion to constantly draw parallels between you and his exes.

Moreover, this recurring behavior might cast doubt on his ability to progress and fully engage in the current relationship. It raises the question of whether he's truly moved on or if recounting these tales is his way of processing his past.

This scenario necessitates careful contemplation as you consider whether his "Exes on Parade" is merely a quirky habit of reminiscing or a sign of lingering issues from

his previous romantic entanglements.

Number Twelve
Selfie Grand Central

"Selfie Grand Central" is not merely a playful moniker—it's a domain where Snap Happy Sasha reigns, her Instagram a testament to self-admiration.

A scroll through the profile is like navigating a sea of selfies, each capturing her best angles and radiating self-assurance.

She embodies the digital era's quintessence, with an online presence that consistently showcases her life, fashion, and accomplishments. Her account serves as a bustling Selfie Grand Central, presenting followers with a never-ending showcase of moments.

The collection of self-portraits is a testament to her self-love and an ongoing quest for validation from her audience.

Amidst the myriad of artfully angled shots, her captions blend wit with trending tags, painting a vivid picture of her world. She thrives on the adoration of her followers, with each like and comment amplifying her online aura.

Snap Happy Sasha's continuous self-display, a hallmark of modern self-confidence, sparks discourse on the thin line between healthy self-esteem and self-obsession. Her focus on herself serves as both a celebration of self-empowerment and a cautionary tale of vanity's subtle allure.

In the grand scheme, her Instagram transcends a mere profile; it's an unabashed declaration of self-adoration in a society that both applauds individuality and examines egotism. Her feed stands as a meticulously curated anthology dedicated to the one she loves most profoundly—herself.

Number Thirteen
Stretching the Truth

"Stretching the Truth" explores the tendencies of an individual, whom we'll call Fibbin' Frank, known for a remarkable flair for reshaping reality to always be the main attraction.

These aren't just minor embellishments; it's a conscious tactic he employs to influence how he is perceived and to keep himself in the spotlight.

He is a maestro of exaggeration, elevating mundane occurrences into riveting narratives that ensnare his audience, painting himself as either the hero or the standout character.

When he recounts events from his day or a

chance meeting, he has a knack for injecting each story with suspense and excitement, making every moment seem more significant than it might truly be.

His penchant for embellishment extends to how he represents his achievements and life stories. He skillfully highlights his successes and glosses over his failures.

It's as though he's curating a persona built on half-truths and exaggerations, all to leave a lasting impression.

His tendency to twist the truth stems from a deep-seated need for acclaim. He craves the spotlight, and by distorting reality, he makes sure he's always at the core of every exchange.

His narratives aren't merely for amusement;

they're calculated moves to enhance his image and cement his place at the center stage.

Initially, his magnetism may draw people in, captivated by his charisma and the allure of his tales. However, over time, this can result in doubts and a sense of distrust among his audience.

Observers who catch on to his pattern might question the veracity of his tales and the sincerity of his persona. It becomes a puzzle to discern the real from the exaggerated, as the line between the two grows ever more blurred.

"Stretching the Truth" with Fibbin' Frank paints a picture of someone whose desire for attention and adulation leads them to warp reality, crafting an identity designed to

captivate, irrespective of the cost to honesty
and realness.

Number Fourteen
The Red-Carpet Dreamer

Meet Vain Vanessa, in her world, she's the unequivocal star, expecting fanfare akin to a celebrity's grand red carpet moment.

The spotlight, she assumes, should be hers by default, anticipating nothing less than the highest degree of adoration and veneration.

She expects you to unfurl the red carpet, ensuring she receives treatment that befits her lavish desires.

Her list of demands is not just lengthy but detailed and uncompromising, borne from a deep-seated belief in her entitlement to special consideration and constant attention.

It's not just the grand gestures; the smallest aspects of her life demand precision. How her coffee is made, the exact temperature she prefers, or even her choice of water—each must align with her precise standards.

From Vanessa's viewpoint, her significance is unrivaled, and she insists on recognition of this fact through the fulfillment of her every dictate.

The level of attentiveness she commands isn't just a preference but a strict prerequisite for the privilege of her presence.

Carrying herself with a distinct air of superiority, she lives as if every exit is a curtain call to thunderous applause.

She depends on you, and indeed everyone in

her orbit, to uphold her self-styled grandeur, endorsing her grandiose self-image, as if she is perpetually center stage.

In essence, Vain Vanessa craves a level of indulgence and allegiance that's typically allotted to the famed, expecting from you a ceaseless exhibition of deference and homage.

Number Fifteen
Jealousy Overload

Watch out – if anyone else seems to capture a sliver of your attention, the green-eyed monster isn't far behind, embodied by Jealous Jerry.

The storm of envy that comes with a Love Bomber's attention is intense. It's not just a brief twinge of envy; it's an emotional whirlwind that upends rational thought with waves of suspicion.

In his view, potential rivals aren't just present; they're perceived as severe threats to his monopoly on your affections.

A simple conversation with someone else can unleash a tempest of emotion in him, revealing not just fleeting insecurity but an all-consuming fire of possessiveness that may begin with a subtle jab and escalate into a full display of jealous fury and demands.

He doesn't just push the boundaries of rationality; he claims dominion over your independence. To him, a mere friendly gesture towards another is seen as a betrayal, prompting a swift demand for your undivided reassurance.

Jealous Jerry's jealousy weaves through the nuances of your daily life, casting shadows over simple interactions and tainting your tranquility with relentless suspicion.

His affection doesn't set you free; it clings and stifles, tightening around you with the demands of his jealousy. He doesn't aim to simply be your choice but your sole focus, the exclusive benefactor of your attention and devotion.

If not addressed, his jealousy doesn't merely damage—it dissolves, steadily eating away at trust and the freedoms vital to a healthy relationship.

His extreme jealousy marks a dangerous skew in the relationship's balance, transforming a potential source of happiness into a burdensome shackle, making each day a battle to keep your head above the flood of his clinginess.

Number Sixteen
Boundaries? What Boundaries?

Personal space isn't a concept she readily acknowledges—Clingy Clare is all about breaching your walls, invited or not.

Imagine a world where the notion of 'personal space' is disregarded, a realm where the boundaries that constitute 'you' are not respected but often invisible to her.

Dealing with her means facing someone who doesn't merely overlook personal boundaries; she seems unaware of their necessity, treating your defenses and personal spaces as mere challenges.

To her, the barriers you set are obstacles to an

ultimate goal: unceasing, uninterrupted access to your world. With persistence and an overwhelming affection, she probes for any gap in your defenses, testing the limits of your personal space with worrisome regularity.

She has a way of making you question your own need for space, masking her intrusions as gestures of love or concern. Such tactics weaken your defenses, making you more vulnerable to her constant presence.

You might find her sifting through your belongings, insisting on being part of every facet of your life, or ignoring your expressed wishes for alone time.

Her perpetual closeness and intense attention, which Clingy Clare sees as expressions of love, actually amount to an invasive overstep.

This behavior is not just suffocating; it contradicts the very essence of a healthy partnership, one that should be built on trust and mutual respect. Someone who dismantles your boundaries like she does is subtly manipulating the dynamics of the relationship.

It's an attempt to dominate, to blur the lines that protect your individuality, your autonomy, and your psychological well-being.

Encountering someone who treats your boundaries as inconsequential or nonexistent, like Clingy Clare, is a significant warning sign. She isn't looking for an equal partner; she wants someone whose sense of self can be overwhelmed with her constant need for closeness.

Boundaries are not negotiable; they are vital. Upholding these limits is key to maintaining your sense of self in any relational dynamic.

Number Seventeen
Expecting the Royal Treatment

They want to be treated like royalty, but don't expect them to return the favor. At slot seventeen, we meet Self-Centered Seth, a figure who is besotted with a rather lopsided idea of affection—one where they are the sun around which all others orbit, basking in a glow of attention they never intend to reflect.

Seth has a self-image so inflated; that he lives for the parade of privileges and affirmations that would typically grace nobility.

His daily routine revolves around a narrative that he is of singular importance, and the world must conform to his whims.

The idea of mutuality is as foreign to him as humility; the scales of balance always tip drastically in his favor.

This person expects a constant stream of praise and service as if it's their due. Yet, when the moment arrives for them to express gratitude or return these favors, their presence is as substantial as a wisp of smoke.

They navigate their relationships with a crown on their head, awaiting applause for every minor deed, insisting on nothing but the finest experiences and possessions.

The basic acts of sharing tasks, providing emotional support, or just being there for others are foreign to Self-Centered Seth unless it directly feeds into his own contentment and ease.

To him, a gesture of kindness is not an act of mutual respect but a tributary flowing into the grandiose river of his ego.

The crux of the issue here lies in the sheer imbalance this entitlement fosters within a relationship. A healthy partnership thrives on a steady rhythm of give-and-take, respecting each other's contributions and presence.

However, those entrenched in the mindset of Seth disrupt this harmony. They view relationships not as a collaborative journey but as a stage for their soliloquy, expecting VIP treatment while offering barely a nod to their partner's needs or sacrifices.

They are enamored not with their partner but

with the pedestal upon which they've placed themselves, casting their wants and pleasures in the starring role while the concept of a partnership languishes in the shadows.

Acknowledging this trait in Self-Centered Seth is pivotal; it often points to an underlying sense of entitlement and emotional disconnect that may signal a hefty emotional price tag for those entangled with such a personality.

Number Eighteen
Flirting with the Crowd

When Charming Charlie, the Love Bomber, weaves her web, the experience is both intoxicating and perilous. Her mastery over the digital space becomes a double-edged sword—one moment, a token of affection, the next, a tool for manipulation.

Her craft is not just flirting with the crowd; it's seducing with intent, drawing you into a whirlwind where the lines between genuine interest and calculated moves are expertly blurred.

The Love Bomber's strategy is to overwhelm with affection, to make you feel like the center of the universe. Charlie excels in this role, her flirtations are both widespread and intensely personal.

You are led to believe that you alone have captured her interest, that the winks and hearts are symbols of a connection that transcends the digital realm.

Yet, the exclusivity is an illusion, a smokescreen that dissipates when you notice the same emojis gracing the comments of others.

Her digital dalliances are a barrage of incoming fire that you're never quite prepared for. The speed and frequency of her messages, the seeming sincerity behind each emoji sent, can be overwhelming.

This is her territory—where Love Bombing is not just about the immediate affection she showers upon you, but also about the constant reminder that her attention is a prize to be won, coveted by many, secured by none.

She utilizes her charm as both a lure and a leash. In the echo chamber of notifications and direct messages, you become accustomed to the sound of her virtual laughter, and the sight of her playful banter.

But the reality is, you're part of a broader audience, participants in a performance where the script is written to keep you hooked, to make you crave the spotlight that she shines indiscriminately.

For those who fall into her trap, the digital

romance is a mirage that promises much but yields little.

The more you invest, the more you realize the return is fleeting. The emojis, the likes, the moments of seemingly undivided attention—they're all part of the show.

And in this show, Charlie is both the star and the director, playing to a full house where everyone is hoping for a solo performance that will never come.

It's essential to recognize this pattern for what it is—a manipulation of your emotional world through the guise of modern flirtation.

Charming Charlie, the Love Bomber, does not seek to build something lasting but to bask in the adoration of the moment, leaving a trail of confusion and unmet expectations.

Her love is as ephemeral as the stories that disappear after 24 hours—a bright streak in the digital sky that burns out before you can even make a wish. Sure, she's flirty with you, but her emojis are flying into others' DMs too.

Number Nineteen
Goes MIA When Mad

The archetype of MIA Mya adds a chilling dynamic to the already complex landscape of Love Bombing.

With her, the high of attention and affection comes with an unspoken threat: the moment displeasure creeps into her view, she retreats into the shadows, cutting off the warmth of her presence and leaving you in a bewildering silence.

Mya's strategy is a form of emotional punishment and control. Her sudden disappearances are not mere coincidences; they are calculated moves designed to invoke anxiety and attachment.

In the dance of closeness and withdrawal, she is a master choreographer. When things are going her way, she's present, her messages flood your inbox, and her interest in your life seems insatiable.

However, this is not a steadfast commitment—it's a conditional one. Her withdrawal is abrupt and total. One minute, she's an active participant in your life, and the next, she's a ghost, her online avatars turning into silent sentinels that mark her absence.

Texts go unanswered, and calls unreturned. The "seen" receipt becomes a digital mark of the emotional limbo she's left you in.

This behavior serves multiple purposes in the

arsenal of a Love Bomber like MIA Mya. Firstly, it's a demonstration of power.

She shows that she can and will withdraw her affections on a whim, which can make you more desperate to regain her attention and less likely to do whatever prompted her disappearance in the first place.

It's a way of training your behavior, reinforcing the cycles that keep you within her emotional grasp.

Secondly, it instills a sense of uncertainty. The unpredictability of her presence keeps you on edge, always wondering if and when she'll return, and what state your relationship will be in when she does.

The relief that comes with her return is

intense, but it's also reinforcing the dynamic, teaching you to associate her presence with the resolution of anxiety, regardless of how that anxiety was created.

Lastly, Mya's vanishing act is a tool for evading confrontation. By going MIA when she's upset, she avoids having to communicate her feelings or work through issues. Instead, she leaves a void that you're left to fill with your own doubts, fears, and desires to fix things.

It's a silent manipulation that turns her displeasure into an emotional black hole, sucking in your peace of mind and leaving you scrambling for a resolution that lies solely in her hands.

The Love Bomber's withdrawal is a tactic as potent as their affection, and with MIA Mya, the pattern of presence and absence is a calculated part of the relationship's rhythm.

Recognizing this pattern is crucial—it's not just about coping with her absences, but understanding the manipulation at play. It's a signal to reassess the health of the connection and consider the long-term implications of such emotional volatility.

If they're upset, they might just disappear, leaving you on read and out in the cold.

Number Twenty
Your Friends Are Ringing Alarm Bells

In the twisted narrative of Love Bombing, there lurks a character often perceived as the villain by the Love Bomber but seen as a guardian by those not under the spell: let's call him Cautionary Craig.

Cautionary Craig is an archetype representing the concerned voices of your friends and family, the ones who aren't dazzled by the fireworks of a Love Bomber's initial charm offensive.

They stand on the periphery, their perspective untainted by the shower of affection and promises that you are receiving, and from this vantage point, they are sounding the alarm loud and clear.

Craig sees through the facade. He doesn't just hear the proclamations of undying love and the soulmate narrative; he watches the actions, the pace, and the pressure.

He notices the Love Bomber's need to monopolize your time and how they push to define the relationship's trajectory on their terms. He sees the red flags for what they are: warning signs of a potentially manipulative and unhealthy partnership.

When your friends, exemplified by Craig, express concern, it's often because the intensity and speed of the relationship's progression seem engineered rather than organic.

They might notice that the Love Bomber's grand gestures are more about demonstrating control than celebrating your connection.

They see that the constant communication isn't just attentiveness, but a strategy to isolate you from your support system. They recognize the extravagant gifts not as acts of generosity but as chains designed to create a sense of obligation.

Your friends might point out that genuine relationships are built on a foundation of mutual respect and understanding that grows over time.

They remind you that love should not feel like a whirlwind that leaves you breathless and disoriented, but more like a steady flame that warms and enlightens.

They're concerned that your autonomy is being overshadowed by the Love Bomber's scripted narrative—a tale where you're not a co-author but a character being written into someone else's story.

Moreover, Cautionary Craig and your inner circle are alarmed by the potential for emotional manipulation.

Love Bombing can be a prelude to gaslighting, where your reality is constantly questioned, and to psychological dependence, where your happiness seems inextricably linked to the bomber's presence and approval.

The Love Bomber's over-the-top affection can easily switch to cold withdrawal as a form of punishment or control, leaving you in a state of confusion and yearning for the return of the Love Bomber's attentions.

When you're the focal point of a Love Bomber's intense courtship, it can be challenging to heed the cautionary advice of friends like Craig. The bomber's allure is strong, their tactics tailored to overwhelm your senses and cloud judgment. But if your inner circle, the people who know you and have your best interests at heart, are consistently expressing concern, it's a critical signal worth listening to.

They're not just ringing alarm bells without cause; they're trying to cut through the noise of the Love Bomber's orchestra. In the complex symphony of human relationships, the discordant notes they point out are meant to preserve the harmony of your life's melody.

Their interventions are acts of care and loyalty, urging you to step back, slow down, and assess the relationship with a clear head and an open heart.

The Love Bomber vs. The Narcissist

For those intrigued by the nuanced distinctions in relationship dynamics, I offer a clear delineation between a Love Bomber and a Narcissist.

When diving into the complexities of relationships, we often come across the terms 'Love Bombing' and 'narcissism'.

Although they might seem similar and sometimes occur together, they are, in reality, distinct with unique patterns and motivations. Grasping these distinctions is key to managing and understanding the challenging dynamics they bring into personal connections.

Love Bombing-What It Is: Imagine someone showering you with affection, attention, and adoration, all in a bid to win your trust and affection swiftly. That's Love Bombing for you.

Breaking It Down-Fast and Furious: Love Bombing hits hard and fast. The person doing this, or the Love Bomber, overwhelms their target with gifts, compliments, and affection.

A Play of Manipulation: There's a calculated angle to Love Bombing. The Love Bomber uses this overwhelming affection to create a sense of need and to gain control over the other person.

Here Today, Gone Tomorrow: Typically, Love Bombing is a start-of-relationship phenomenon, and it often fades away once the Love Bomber feels secure in the relationship.

From Highs to Lows: The intense affection experienced during Love Bombing is hard to maintain, and its eventual drop-off can leave the target feeling confused and emotionally upset.

Narcissism-What It Is: Narcissism is a personality trait marked by an inflated sense of self, an insatiable need for attention and admiration, and a lack of empathy towards others.

Breaking It Down: Long-Term Scenario: Unlike Love Bombing, narcissism isn't a phase; it's a deep-rooted personality trait that shows up consistently across various aspects of a person's life and relationships.

All About Me: Narcissists have their eyes firmly set on their own needs and interests, seeking validation and admiration to boost their ego.

Empathy, Not Their Strong Suit: They find it tough to relate to or understand others' feelings, leading to behavior that can come off as insensitive or manipulative.

Power Play: Narcissists often seek control and dominance, looking for positions that put them in power.

Finding the Line-Love Bombing and narcissism can appear together, but they aren't identical. A Narcissist may use Love Bombing as a tool, but Love Bombing can also come from those without Narcissistic tendencies.

The main difference? Narcissism is a long-lasting trait, while Love Bombing is an intense but usually brief phase.

Understanding these nuances helps people recognize and navigate these behaviors in relationships, ensuring they protect their well-being and move towards healthier, balanced connections.

In today's complex world of dating and relationships, a deceptive and manipulative behavior known as "Love Bombing" has come to the forefront, bringing with it a range of deep impacts on those searching for genuine connection and love.

At its very heart, Love Bombing is all about showering someone with intense affection, attention, and praise, all with the goal of quickly gaining their trust and affection.

It might look like grand romantic gestures or passionate declarations of love at first, making it seem like a dream come true.

But underneath this layer of passion and devotion, there's a darker side filled with manipulation, control, and psychological tactics. The emotional and psychological effects of being on the receiving end of Love Bombing are immense. People might find themselves caught up in a whirlwind of romance, completely oblivious to the manipulative strategies at play.

The person employing Love Bombing is often trying to create a sense of dependency and affect the other person's self-esteem, independence, and ability to make sound decisions about the relationship.

This emotional turmoil can leave deep scars, leading to feelings of confusion, betrayal, and a reduced sense of self-worth, even after the relationship is over.

Catching the signs of Love Bombing early on in a relationship is crucial. It allows people to safeguard their emotional health, hold onto their independence, and pursue relationships that are built on true affection, respect, and shared growth.

This book is here to shed light on the hidden aspects of Love Bombing and narcissism, arming readers with the knowledge and tools they need to spot and navigate these challenging situations.

By delving into the strategies used by those who Love Bomb, understanding the psychological harm they cause, and learning how to protect oneself and develop healthy, equal relationships, this book stands as an essential guide for anyone navigating today's intricate world of dating and relationships.

Unpacking Love Bombing:-Love Bombing is essentially a deceptive strategy where an individual showers their partner with extraordinary levels of affection, praise, and adoration, all with the ulterior motive to manipulate and dominate them.

This intense flood of romantic gestures and

loving words takes place right at the onset of the relationship, creating a strong emotional bond. This deliberate act seeks to win over the trust and dependence of the person on the receiving end.

The Backstory and Psychological Roots-The phrase "Love Bombing" found its origins in the 1970s, coined by the Unification Church in the United States as they described their technique of converting new members.

Devotees would overwhelm newcomers with love and acceptance, cultivating a sense of community and influencing their belief system. This term has since evolved, now also referencing a similar manipulative tactic within romantic relationships.

From a psychological standpoint, Love Bombing is often linked to a variety of personality disorders, including but not limited to Narcissistic personality disorder, borderline personality disorder, and antisocial personality disorder.

Those who resort to Love Bombing typically harbor an overwhelming need for control and affirmation, which is usually a reflection of profound internal insecurities and a fragile self-esteem.

Aims and Driving Forces-The predominant objective of Love Bombing is to establish control and dominance over the targeted individual.

The Love Bomber crafts an intense and fast-paced romance, striving to make their partner feel extraordinarily cherished and indispensable. This deep connection paves the way for manipulation and control, satisfying the Love Bomber's craving for dominance and acknowledgment.

Those who engage in Love Bombing are driven by various underlying motives, encompassing a quest for authority, a hunger for admiration, and a tendency to conceal their vulnerabilities.

Utilizing Love Bombing as a strategy, they seek to quickly instill a sense of commitment and security in the relationship, making it challenging for the targeted individual to stay objective and maintain their autonomy.

To truly comprehend Love Bombing, one must

delve into its definition, historical roots, and the psychological mechanisms that propel individuals to partake in this manipulative conduct.

By exploring the objectives and motivations that underlie Love Bombing, we are better equipped to identify these harmful patterns in relationships, paving the way towards nurturing healthier and more equitable partnerships.

Navigating the Tempest
Recognizing and Resisting Love Bombing in New Relationships

Entering the early stages of a romantic endeavor is undeniably thrilling. The rush of new affection, the promise of potential love—it's all exhilarating.

Yet, in this intoxicating phase, it's vital to remain vigilant, especially when the relationship emits the early signs of Love Bombing.

It's a time when your alertness to these signals is most crucial, providing you with the knowledge and tools necessary to discern the worrisome from the genuine.

At the beginning of a potential Love Bombing situation, one might drown in an overwhelming tide of praise. A person employing these tactics often showers their target with excessive compliments, creating a surreal environment that seems too good to be true.

This overabundance isn't simply flattery; it's a deliberate strategy to rapidly gain trust and affection. Recognizing the difference between sincere admiration and manipulative praise is critical at this juncture because the latter is a hallmark of Love Bombing.

The psychological impact of a continuous stream of compliments can lead to the 'halo effect,' where the Love Bomber appears in an unreasonably favorable light, causing you to overlook possible flaws and red flags.

To maintain a level head amidst this whirlwind, it's essential to develop strategies for emotional strength, such as routine self-reflection, mindfulness practices, and cultivating a strong support network.

It's also important to scrutinize the timing and intent behind the praise. Are these compliments genuine, or are they aimed at influencing your decisions?

Cultivating discernment can help maintain emotional independence. Alongside this, preserving your personal space, nurturing your interests, and upholding your boundaries are vital steps in protecting your sense of self.

Moreover, learning about healthy relationship dynamics and emotional manipulation tactics can deepen your understanding, helping you differentiate between overwhelming generosity and genuine kindness.

If needed, seeking professional help can provide tailored guidance, while connecting with others who've shared similar experiences can offer valuable support.

Grand gestures and lavish gifts can also be a part of Love Bombing, creating a fairy tale scenario that may lead to a sense of obligation and hastened relationship development.

It's necessary to lift the veil on these displays and understand their true intentions, which often revolve around establishing control and creating emotional dependence.

In the whirlwind that follows, emotions can escalate, and perceptions can become skewed, making it difficult to see the relationship clearly.

The Love Bomber's aim is to create an illusion of security and commitment, manipulating your feelings and perceptions to their advantage. When the grandeur eventually subsides, the aftermath can leave you struggling to regain independence and clarity.

Equipped with the understanding of Love Bombing's true motives and psychological intricacies, you're now empowered to approach new relationships with a clear mind and a resilient heart.

Recognizing these warning signs is paramount to protecting your emotional well-being and ensuring that the affection you give and receive is as authentic as it is heartfelt.

In writing this book, my aim has been to empower you to forge your own path, one that's marked by strength and clear boundaries—a path that upholds the essence of who you truly are, even amidst the whirlwind of a phenomenon like Love Bombing.

I understand that simply being aware of Love Bombing isn't enough; it requires you to dig deep and muster a robust inner strength, coupled with an unwavering determination to protect the sacred space that is your personal life.

I have crafted this book as a tool to help you nurture resilience and to clearly define the protective borders that guard your unique sense of self. Within these pages, I encourage you to "Embrace Your Inner Fortitude." It's a call for you to stand firm in recognizing your inherent worth, a worth that is not, and should never be, contingent on someone else's affirmation or material offerings.

I stress the importance of looking back at your past encounters to seek out patterns that can inform and fortify your stand against future instances of Love Bombing.

Creating a nurturing circle of friends and engaging in practices that foster self-care and presence of mind are key elements in developing the emotional robustness you need. Moreover, it's critical to delineate and assert your personal boundaries with confidence, and to consistently honor your core values through maintaining your own interests and regular self-reflection.

While learning about Love Bombing I hope to arm you with the knowledge necessary to recognize the signs and long-term impacts of this deceptive strategy, thus serving as a shield against manipulative tactics.

The ability to analyze underlying intentions and to trust your intuition is emphasized, as these are vital tools in your psychological armor.

By adopting these strategies, you're not just surviving; you're thriving in the face of Love Bombing's complexities. You're claiming your right to independence and paving the way towards relationships that are equally nourishing and balanced—an investment in the emotional wealth of your future.

Love Bombers have an incessant drive to maintain a constant presence in your life, a tactic that often masquerades as concern but is, in reality, a manipulative snare.

The pressure of their relentless communication can be taxing, leading to anxiety and an erosion of your autonomy. This is why I stress the importance of setting and honoring healthy communication boundaries, which includes valuing your own time and space, trusting your instincts when communication feels intrusive, and building a network of support outside the Love Bomber's sphere of influence.

Taking control of your personal space and establishing a balanced pattern of communication is essential to liberate yourself from the clutches of a Love Bomber.

Remember, true autonomy is your right, and genuine, healthy relationships should bolster, not overwhelm, your sense of self.

When you first find yourself the cynosure of someone's unyielding attention, it's easy to be swept up in the thrill of it all. The persistent messages and affirmations of love may at first seem to be heartfelt tokens of someone's affection.

Yet, as time unfolds, you come to see that these gestures are double-edged, at once enchanting and a means of exerting control.

Consider the early stages: a cascade of texts and calls that make you feel seen and valued. Such attention from a Love Bomber is heady and can weave a strong emotional bond that seems both precious and exclusive.

But as days pass, what was once sweet can sour, turning caring attentiveness into a suffocating bind. The relentless nature of their communication begins to wear on you, no longer feeling like love, but rather a shackle disguised as devotion.

This constant contact is a tactic of dominance, designed to pull you away from your support systems, leaving you dependent on the Love Bomber. It can be unsettling to realize that your newfound partner is not simply involved in your life but is beginning to dictate it.

With every message and every call, your autonomy seems to slip further away, leaving you feeling watched and controlled. This loss of independence often comes with an emotional cost, chipping away at your self-esteem and sense of self-reliance.

It's crucial to recognize these behaviors for what they are: strategies of control rather than genuine care. Drawing firm boundaries is not just necessary; it's an act of self-preservation.

To dismantle the Love Bomber's hold over you requires fortitude, the courage to assert your right to space and privacy, and the strength to reconnect with your own values and needs.

Addressing the urgency a Love Bomber places on commitment is another aspect that demands your attention. They often push for exclusivity or a serious commitment prematurely to secure their influence in your life. Understanding why they're so insistent on this rush and learning to set the relationship's tempo on your terms is crucial to keeping your independence intact.

One of the most nefarious strategies employed by Love Bombers is isolation—systematically undermining your relationships with friends and family to ensure they become the sole focus of your world.

Recognizing and resisting this tactic is vital for maintaining a support network that can help you navigate out of the Love Bomber's sphere of influence.

As you move through the journey of reclaiming your independence and resilience, remember that the early signs of Love Bombing are not to be ignored. They serve as warning beacons, highlighting the need for vigilance in preserving the equilibrium of your relationships.

This chapter isn't just a collection of observations; it's a tool designed to arm you with the wisdom to discern genuine affection from manipulation, allowing you to forge connections that are healthy, reciprocal, and truly enriching.

Twenty Unmistakable Signs You're with a Narcissist

Number One
Grandiosity

Within the intricate web of a Narcissist's psyche, they erect a grandiose pedestal for themselves, soaring above the masses.

As if a monarch of their own making, they reside in a world where they alone are celebrated for their imagined superiority.

Let's take a journey to the core of such grandiosity—a fundamental aspect of Narcissistic psychology. We'll gently lift the curtain on the Narcissist's supposed superiority, critically examining the excessive self-regard and often the hidden vulnerabilities that drive their behavior.

To grasp the full picture of a Narcissist's grandiose nature, it's essential to look at its roots. This inflated sense of self often stems from a contradictory upbringing where excessive praise failed to meet an emotional void, leaving a raw wound that was never truly addressed.

The grandiosity we observe is less of an identity and more of a bandage covering this deep-seated trauma, serving as armor against a world they perceive as belittling.

The performance of grandiosity is the most overt symptom of the Narcissist's inner narrative.

With theatrical flair, they exhibit their supposed brilliance, flaunting achievements and talents that, upon closer inspection, are frequently exaggerated or entirely fabricated.

This isn't just theatrics for theatrics' sake—it's a desperate cry for the acknowledgment and importance they crave.

When one dares to question the Narcissist's grand narrative, the encounter is often surreal, as if you're grappling with a mirage.

Any challenge to their self-image is met with a spectrum of responses, from dismissive coldness to volatile anger.

It's a reflex to protect the fragile edifice of their self-perception, which cannot withstand the scrutiny of reality.

The Narcissist's grandiosity exacts a high toll on those closest to them. Relationships become one-sided, with the Narcissist expecting constant admiration and subservience to their needs.

Others are merely players in the grand drama of their life, valued only for their ability to reinforce the Narcissist's grandiose self-image.

If you find yourself within the orbit of a Narcissist's grandiose world, maintaining self-awareness and firm personal boundaries is crucial. Recognize their displays for what they are—a façade.

Understanding that their actions reflect their insecurities, not your worth, can empower you to interact with poise and self-respect.

The grandiosity seen in narcissism is a complicated construct, acting as both a bulwark and a cell for the Narcissist.

As we pull away the grand veil, we not only expose a mechanism for control but also a silent, desperate bid for validation.

With this understanding, we can approach such individuals with a balanced blend of empathy and caution, safeguarding our well-being while acknowledging the concealed pain beneath their ostentatious display.

Number Two
Fantasies of Success

In the shadowy recesses of a Narcissist's psyche lies a dreamscape where grandeur and omnipotence are not aspirations but certainties. This is not the realm of fleeting whimsy we all know but a foundational part of their identity.

Their relentless pursuit of unprecedented success isn't about setting and achieving goals but an unquenchable thirst for a victory so grand that it defies comparison.

Imagine the Narcissist as the protagonist of an epic tale they've authored, where they stand as a colossus of achievement and influence, basking in the glow of their imagined monumental feats. Such fancies are not confined to their private moments; they are ever-present, dictating the plot of their waking life.

Power for them is not a means to an end but the end itself—an unyielding power that places them at the helm, commanding life's tides without opposition. Their narrative is steeped in a conviction of their ordained right to rule, to bend reality to their iron will.

To the Narcissist, their brilliance and allure are not traits they strive to cultivate; they see them as intrinsic, as due entitlements.

They craft tales where their intellect shines with unrivaled luster, and their allure captivates all, a ceaseless fountain of praise and adoration.

When it comes to love, they envision a romance that isn't grounded in the realities of partnership but rather in finding a mirror—a counterpart to reflect and amplify the love they reserve for themselves. They crave a love that is less about depth and connection and more about validating their own grandiosity.

These flights of fancy are not mere mental diversions; they're crucial to the Narcissist's self-image.

They serve as armor against the arrows of doubt and insecurity, a fortress safeguarding a core that is surprisingly fragile.

Interacting with a Narcissist means

navigating a landscape defined by these illusions. Should the harsh light of reality seep in, challenging the grandeur of their fantasies, it often unleashes a storm of disarray and indignation, the backlash of which is borne by those closest to them.

The stark contrast between the Narcissist's illusory world and the everyday is a source of constant tension.

Their fantastical narrative stands at odds with the tangible, often unremarkable nature of real life, hindering genuine connections and the pursuit of actual fulfillment.

This chasm between illusion and reality sets the stage for a life of dissonance, a life where the truth is not an ally but an unwelcome intruder,

ever threatening to unravel the grand tapestry

of their imagined existence.

Number Three
Need for Admiration

In the realm of the Narcissist's psyche, the quest for admiration is a relentless and voracious drive, akin to an unquenchable thirst. This intense longing for affirmation goes beyond a mere wish; it forms a critical pillar supporting their sense of self and inflating their ego with much-needed air.

Delving into the nuances of this trait reveals the Narcissist's identity to be largely constructed on external validation. They are dependent on the world around them to provide the accolades they are unable to cultivate internally.

To them, acknowledgment from others isn't a luxury; it's an essential need. Mirroring the dependency of an actor on an audience's acclaim, the Narcissist seeks a perpetual chorus of praise to affirm their existence and bolster their self-perception.

This profound need manifests in the Narcissist's every action. They are prone to casting out lures for compliments, or manipulating scenarios to ensure their perceived uniqueness is celebrated.

They transform their environment—be it the office, their online presence, or their personal sphere—into a stage where they are the star, awaiting the adulation, the digital likes, the affirming comments, and the accolades they believe they deserve.

When conversing, a Narcissist will often pivot the spotlight back onto themselves, keeping the dialogue centered around their person. They frequently boast, sometimes stretching the truth to its limits, to portray themselves in an extraordinary light.

Their narrated achievements are not just stories; they are epics meant to solidify their place on a pedestal above the rest.

It's critical to recognize, however, that their search for admiration transcends the mere feeding of their ego. At its core, it's a shield against an underlying ocean of insecurities and the dread of mediocrity.

Each slice of praise serves as a temporary

salve to these hidden fears, but it's a solution that never lasts, prompting an endless cycle of validation-seeking.

The toll of this incessant demand for admiration is most heavily borne by those in the Narcissist's orbit. Relationships may turn into exhausting endeavors, as they become marathons of emotional support, with the Narcissist's need for validation as the finish line that keeps moving farther away.

Fail to supply the expected level of esteem, and one might be met with harsh criticism or outright dismissal. For those who must navigate the tricky waters of interaction with a Narcissist, understanding this compulsive need for admiration is vital.

Discerning between healthy self-respect and a pathological hunger for validation aids in setting realistic boundaries and managing one's own emotional resources.

In dealing with a Narcissist, the challenge lies in offering empathy for their needs while safeguarding your personal emotional sanctuary. The Narcissist's pursuit of admiration is a dance of self-elevation and a defense against the fear of insignificance.

Recognizing this critical interplay within the Narcissist's relationships is imperative, as it is a predominant theme of their interpersonal engagements and a key to upholding one's mental well-being amidst their ceaseless quest for accolades.

Number Four
Sense of Entitlement

Entitlement, for the Narcissist, isn't just a trait; it is their unwritten law of existence. They carry within them an unshakeable conviction that they are due special treatment, a belief not consciously chosen but embedded into the fabric of their identity.

This discussion seeks to decode the enigma of Narcissistic entitlement and its pervasive influence on their relationships and behavior.

Picture the Narcissist as a monarch of old, donning an unseen crown, walking amongst the masses with the air of someone above the common fray.

They don't just feel—they know—that their needs and desires should naturally eclipse those of others. This isn't up for debate; in the narrative of their life, it is an unassailable truth.

This sense of entitlement can be observed in the most mundane to the most momentous aspects of life. For the Narcissist, jumping the queue or commanding attention isn't just a whim, it's expected due.

In intimate partnerships, their word is often law, their partner's needs relegated to mere footnotes. In professional settings, the entitlement narrative continues. Narcissists may assume promotions and accolades are their due, regardless of merit or workplace etiquette.

They believe their ideas should automatically be embraced, their directions followed without question, setting the stage for inevitable workplace drama.

This skewed perspective extends to a belief that they are exempt from the rules that govern the rest.

Narcissists often think they can shortcut through life's procedures and protocols, leading to a blatant disregard for societal norms and, occasionally, legality.

Their entitlement often blinds them to the concept of mutual respect and personal boundaries.

At its essence, a Narcissist's entitlement is a

denial of others' independence and value—a world molded to their wishes, where they are the ultimate authority.

It's more than an attitude; it's the lens through which they view all life's interactions and transactions.

Such an ingrained sense of entitlement doesn't come without cost. It often results in a wake of damaged relationships and conflicts, as the Narcissist's expectations repeatedly collide with the principles of mutual respect and social give-and-take.

Those in the Narcissist's orbit often find themselves grappling with this entitlement, leading to exhaustive negotiations and frequently, one-sided sacrifices.

Recognizing this trait in Narcissists is pivotal for those who deal with them. It involves acknowledging that this behavior stems from a need for dominance and control and crafting strategies to manage it effectively.

Boundaries need to be drawn with care and upheld steadfastly to prevent relationships from devolving into a series of unjust concessions to the Narcissist's insatiable demands.

Ultimately, the sense of entitlement that Narcissists harbor goes beyond being merely disagreeable—it defines their interaction with the world and shapes how they treat others.

Addressing this entitlement with decisiveness and integrity is critical in preserving a functional dynamic in any form of relationship with a Narcissist.

Number Five
Exploitative

Beneath a surface that often sparkles with allure and feigned concern, there lurks a more calculating disposition in some individuals—a predisposition for exploitation that is not merely a quirk but the very pillar of their interaction with others.

Such individuals, marked by a notable lack of genuine empathy, engage with the world around them with a single-minded focus: to propel their personal agendas forward, irrespective of the toll it may take on anyone else.

For those with such a mindset, the concept of

mutual respect and the recognition of others' rights are often alarmingly absent from their considerations. People are not seen as individuals with their own lives and stories but rather as instruments to be played in the grand concert of their ambitions.

Others' emotions, aspirations, or problems are mere background noise, secondary to the all-consuming pursuit of their goals.

Their methods are often subtle, sometimes barely perceptible, as they siphon value from those they encounter—whether it's emotional support, financial gain, or social leverage.

The impact of such exploitation becomes glaringly clear within personal relationships. Here, the connection is not born from mutual respect or affection but from calculated choice, with the other party often being unaware of their assigned role.

It's a chess game where the unsuspecting are maneuvered for the Narcissist's benefit—to enhance their image, expand their resources, or unlock doors to new realms of influence.

This approach bleeds into professional spaces as well, where they might co-opt the work of others, manipulate their way up the corporate ladder, or deflect their own failures onto unsuspecting colleagues.

The fallout from these actions—be it the emotional distress of a deceived partner, the stunted career of a co-worker, or the tarnished reputation of an adversary—is of little concern to them.

Their eyes remain firmly on the prize, the consequences to others merely a passing concern, unworthy of serious consideration in their pursuit of personal glory.

Those who encounter such exploitative individuals often emerge from the experience with a sense of disillusionment. Interactions that once held the promise of reciprocity deteriorate into transactions where they find themselves depleted, the Narcissist having extracted what they needed and moved on.

For someone entering such a dynamic with honest intentions, this realization—that their value to the Narcissist was always measured by their utility—can be particularly painful.

Recognizing these patterns is crucial when dealing with a Narcissist. Establishing clear boundaries, maintaining a strong sense of self-respect, and exercising caution with the trust one extends are essential to avoiding manipulation.

Moreover, it's important for those who have been exploited to understand that the fault lies with the exploiter's inability to empathize or to conduct themselves with integrity—not with the exploited's value as a person.

In essence, exploitation is not just a tactic but an integral part of the Narcissist's interaction with the world, driven by a self-centered agenda and marked by a profound disregard for the wellbeing of others.

Armed with an understanding of this disturbing truth, individuals can better prepare themselves to avoid becoming mere tools in a Narcissist's self-serving plot.

Number Six
Lack of Empathy

In the nuanced spectrum of human personality, a pronounced lack of empathy is often a defining trait of those with Narcissistic tendencies.

This deficiency in emotional intelligence may manifest as either a distinct inability to empathize or a willful refusal to tune into the emotional world of others, leading to a pattern of relational conflict that is emblematically Narcissistic.

Empathy is the emotional thread that connects us, allowing us to not just recognize but also feel the emotional states of our peers.

Yet, within the Narcissistic psyche, this thread is often frayed or entirely missing. Such individuals may exhibit a perplexing detachment from the emotional climates of those around them, sometimes coming across as disinterested or dismissive of the distress and happiness of others.

For someone with Narcissistic characteristics, the inner landscapes and emotional boundaries of others seldom register as priorities.

They may react to the vulnerability or suffering of others with a startling coolness or visible irritation, deeming such emotional expressions as overblown or even a sign of frailty, particularly when they interfere with their own objectives.

This empathetic void can lead to a form of social myopia where the Narcissist remains blind to the emotional signals that enable mutual and supportive human interaction.

In romantic partnerships, this can create an emotional chasm, with the Narcissist often appearing disconnected and unable to genuinely participate in a shared emotional journey.

This empathy gap can extend into actions that are actively harmful. Bereft of an emotional compass, the Narcissist may engage in manipulation, exploitation, or emotional bullying without a trace of regret.

In extreme cases, their response to another

person's misfortune might be grossly inappropriate—untouched by the typical human response to another's pain, they may react with anger, annoyance, or even a disconcerting pleasure.

The incapacity to genuinely engage with the emotions of others not only sabotages the Narcissist's prospects for deep and meaningful relationships but also wraps them in a solitary bubble, where only their needs and feelings are given any real credence.

This leads to a life punctuated by fleeting and unsatisfying connections, devoid of the richness that true empathetic engagement can bring.

For those who find themselves in the orbit of

a person with such a stark lack of empathy, the interaction can be bewildering and hurtful.

It is a complex reality to accept that such a fundamental lack of emotional connection is less a deliberate choice and more a feature of the Narcissist's emotional wiring.

Recognizing the need to safeguard one's own emotional health in the face of this empathy void is crucial, as is understanding that this deficit is a constraint of the Narcissist's emotional capacity, shaping how they perceive and interact with the world at large.

Number Seven
Envy

Envy, a pervasive element among those with Narcissistic inclinations, is more than a transient feeling of desire for what others have; it is an enduring sentiment that permeates their view of themselves and their interactions with the world.

It's not just a matter of wanting what others have; it's a fundamental aspect of their psyche that can both motivate and torment them.

Such individuals often cast a covetous gaze upon the successes and possessions of others, burning with a silent resentment for not having the same.

This grudging attitude may lead them to behave spitefully toward those they envy, attempting to diminish the value of others' achievements or even actively working to sabotage them.

Their ambition is not just to equal but to eclipse the attainments of those around them, often leading to an overblown sense of competition.

Conversely, they tend to view themselves as the frequent target of envy. In their minds, their attributes, victories, or belongings are coveted by all, reinforcing their self-perceived superiority.

This belief can take many forms, from a pronounced display of their success to interpreting benign behavior as envious spite. Such perceptions often serve to bolster their already inflated ego and justify their disdain or dismissive attitude toward others.

This fixation on envy not only affects the Narcissist's relationships, fostering a contentious and suspicious environment, but also fuels a chronic dissatisfaction within them.

They are caught in a loop of perpetual longing, where each new acquisition or accolade only heightens the hunger for more. This unquenchable thirst for more prestige, wealth, or acknowledgment can lead to a life of constant striving but little fulfillment.

The dynamic of envy in Narcissistic individuals sets up a world steeped in rivalry and comparison. It creates a battleground where there are no allies, only adversaries and potential usurpers.

This can result in a lonely existence, deprived of the richness that comes from genuine human connections built on mutual respect and shared joy.

For those interacting with someone driven by envy, it is essential to understand this underlying force.

It can elucidate the often puzzling, antagonistic, or competitive nature of their actions.

By grasping the roots of such behavior, one can better manage their relationship with a Narcissistic individual, safeguarding their emotional health while maintaining a realistic

perspective on the nature of the interaction.

Number Eight
Arrogance

Arrogance is a defining trait in many Narcissistic personalities, revealing itself not merely as intermittent overconfidence but rather as a pervasive attitude that infiltrates the Narcissist's very being and their dealings with others.

Central to arrogance is an exaggerated self-regard, a belief in one's own exceptionalism that overshadows the perspectives and contributions of others.

Narcissists often exhibit an unmerited confidence, dominating conversations and imposing their viewpoints with an air of absolute authority. Their dialogue is marked by an unshakeable belief in their correctness and a propensity to dismiss or devalue alternate opinions as inconsequential or misguided.

Narcissists express their arrogance in myriad ways, ranging from blatant disparagement of others to more insidious forms of disdain.

They might consistently interrupt or redirect conversations to keep the spotlight on themselves, or they may critique others' thoughts with irony or condescension.

Within groups, they often assume the role of the unchallenged leader, pushing their agenda under the guise of being the most capable or knowledgeable.

This trait deeply impacts personal

relationships, where the Narcissist may refuse to recognize or empathize with another's emotional state.

They are likely to meet criticism with antagonism, viewing it as an affront to their perceived faultlessness rather than a chance for personal growth. Their inability to concede to mistakes or express genuine remorse is in stark contrast with their inflated self-image.

Arrogance also stifles the Narcissist's personal growth. Their reluctance to acknowledge personal flaws can halt their development, as they often avoid experiences that might challenge their self-concept.

This stubbornness can lead to a life punctuated by grandiose delusions, increasingly detached from the tangible realities that confront them.

In societal settings, the Narcissist's arrogance can be alienating and stir up discord. Their inclination to belittle those they consider beneath them can make professional or social collaboration challenging, frequently resulting in estrangement or disputes.

For those who must interact with Narcissistic individuals, it's important to understand that their arrogance stems from a deep-seated need to feel superior.

Recognizing this can shed light on the often perplexing nature of their actions. While it can be tough to maintain a relationship with such individuals, setting firm boundaries and cultivating a robust sense of self-respect are essential in managing the tricky dynamics their arrogance creates.

Number Nine
Manipulative

Narcissists often exhibit a behavioral tendency to manipulate those around them, a trait that becomes particularly evident in the way they commandeer conversations and control situations to ensure they remain the focal point.

This need to manipulate is rooted in their deep-seated desire for attention and validation. When engaged in dialogue, these individuals may artfully redirect the topic, no matter how unrelated it might be, back to themselves.

Whether through a clever comment or a strategic interruption, they're adept at hijacking the discourse so that all roads lead back to their own stories, grievances, or achievements.

It's a strategic ploy that's not merely about leading the conversation but about siphoning the collective attention of the group to feed their ego.

This proclivity for manipulation extends beyond mere conversation into the realm of social strategy.

A Narcissist may craft circumstances that shine a spotlight on them, whether by casting themselves in the role of the hero in a narrative or by precipitating a crisis that ensures they receive the support and focus of everyone involved.

Their ability to pull the social strings stems from a sharp insight into interpersonal dynamics, which they exploit to maintain their perceived status and importance.

This manipulative behavior also serves a deeper psychological purpose: their incessant quest for adoration and affirmation.

A Narcissist is often driven by an insatiable need to be at the center of it all, employing various tactics to secure this position.

They might resort to playing the victim to gain sympathy or pretend to be in need of help, all maneuvers carefully calculated to engender concern and maintain their grip on the attention of others, thereby bolstering their sense of self-worth.

In more intimate settings, such as personal relationships, this manipulative tendency can be quite destructive. By constantly steering the attention back to themselves, they neglect and override the needs and feelings of their partners, leading to a one-sided relationship dynamic where the Narcissist's desires take precedence over everything else.

Recognizing the manipulative tactics of a Narcissist is crucial for those who regularly interact with them.

Understanding these strategies can equip individuals with the necessary tools to emotionally insulate themselves from being exploited or emotionally depleted.

Being aware of such manipulative patterns

also allows for the establishment of firm boundaries to counteract the Narcissist's self-absorbed machinations.

Number Ten
Demanding

Narcissists are often known for their high expectations and uncompromising standards, which they impose on those around them.

This trait is not confined to any one area of their lives; it is pervasive, impacting their personal and professional relationships.

Their belief in their own centrality and superiority fuels a conviction that their way of doing things is not only the best but the only way.

These individuals hold a strong sense of entitlement, expecting others to cater to their needs and whims. In their view, their opinions and methods hold primacy over all others, and as such, they expect those in their circle to align with their directives.

Whether it's a specific way a task must be completed or an insistence on certain behaviors or attitudes in social settings, Narcissists demand adherence to their prescribed way of life.

Their demands often leave little room for discussion or deviation. Any attempt to diverge from their prescribed path is typically seen not as a difference in opinion but as a direct challenge to their perceived superiority.

Those who live, work, or associate with Narcissists may find themselves constantly striving to meet these high expectations, frequently at the expense of their own comfort and well-being.

This demanding nature can wreak havoc on personal relationships, creating a lopsided dynamic where the needs of the Narcissist overshadow all others. Partners may find themselves diminishing their own needs or changing themselves in fundamental ways to appease the Narcissist's demands, often leading to personal unhappiness and resentment.

In the workplace, Narcissistic demands can be just as disruptive. A Narcissist may expect their colleagues and subordinates to perform to their exacting standards without consideration for realistic deadlines, workload, or the overall culture of the workplace.

This can create an environment rife with tension, stress, and a high rate of burnout or employee turnover.

Recognizing and understanding the demanding nature of a Narcissist is critical for those who interact with them. It's important for individuals to maintain their own well-being by setting boundaries and clearly communicating their limits.

While it might be daunting to stand up to a Narcissist's high-handed demands, doing so can be essential to prevent an unhealthy dynamic from taking root.

Number Eleven
Controlling

In both their personal and work lives, certain individuals who exhibit Narcissistic qualities can have a profound and often destructive need to exert control.

This compulsion is rooted in a deep desire for dominance, coupled with an intense aversion to feeling exposed or at the mercy of unforeseen circumstances.

Their behavior is characterized by an overarching intent to keep the reins firmly in their hands, ensuring that their environment and the individuals within it reflect their preferences and operate according to their set parameters.

Within the sphere of intimate relationships, the impact of such a controlling nature can be particularly oppressive. These individuals may overstep boundaries to an extreme, dictating their partner's wardrobe, social engagements, and even career trajectory.

The guise of concern or claiming to know best serves as their cover, but the underlying objective is to exert unwavering influence over their partner's life choices.

The result is often a stifling relationship where one person is left with scant room for personal decision-making or self-expression, constantly under the threat of disapproval or punitive measures.

In the realm of work, the presence of a Narcissistic individual who seeks control can be just as harmful. They tend to micromanage their teams, demanding to be consulted on every decision, no matter how trivial.

This iron grip can quash team members' creative and independent spirits, creating a workplace culture where new ideas and initiative are met with resistance or penalization.

Colleagues in such environments frequently feel their contributions are minimized and their ability to work autonomously is under constant challenge.

At the heart of this urge to control is a deep-seated insecurity within the Narcissist, a fear that without such control, they may be exposed to failure or forced to face the chaos of unpredictability – situations they associate with personal weakness.

It's critical for those who deal with such individuals to identify these controlling tendencies. Doing so often involves the establishment of strong personal boundaries and a commitment to maintaining one's autonomy.

This can sometimes mean seeking out the understanding and support of those who grasp the intricacies of such challenging interactions.

Although it can be taxing to navigate a relationship with a controlling Narcissist, putting in place clear boundaries is a vital step in safeguarding one's independence and mental

health.

Number Twelve
Sensitive to Criticism

Narcissistic individuals are often markedly thin-skinned when it comes to receiving criticism. This isn't just a minor irritation for them; it's a deep-seated incapacity to process critiques constructively.

Such individuals may react with explosive anger or overt scorn that seems disproportionate to the feedback given, often leaving others bewildered by the intensity of their response.

This hair-trigger reactivity to criticism has its roots in the Narcissist's inflated ego and self-concept. In their view, to critique them is not to offer a pathway to improvement, but rather to challenge their very sense of self.

Any suggestion of a flaw or mistake is met with a full-frontal defense, escalating what could be a calm exchange into a volatile confrontation.

The merest hint of disapproval is perceived as a personal attack, triggering a defensive posture that is fierce and often intimidating.

Furthermore, Narcissists may deploy scorn as a shield against feeling diminished by criticism. Responding with derision allows them to undermine the person offering the critique, thus deflecting attention away from their own vulnerabilities.

They might cast aspersions on the critic's

abilities or motives, effectively turning the tables and reclaiming the upper hand.

This aversion to criticism represents a formidable obstacle in both personal and professional spheres for the Narcissist. It can shut down healthy dialogue and rob them of opportunities to learn and evolve.

Those in the Narcissist's orbit learn to tread lightly, often resorting to tact and diplomacy to provide feedback without igniting a defensive explosion.

Recognizing and understanding a Narcissist's fragile tolerance for criticism is vital for those who must interact with them. Acknowledging the underlying insecurity that drives their reactions can inform a more empathetic yet firm approach.

It is possible to engage constructively with a Narcissist by framing feedback carefully, but it is also necessary to establish firm boundaries to protect oneself from the fallout of their sometimes volatile reactions.

Number Thirteen
Belittling Others

Narcissistic individuals often employ the tactic of belittling those around them as a means to maintain and elevate their own status.

This behavior is not sporadic or accidental; it's a conscious strategy designed to showcase themselves as more intelligent, skilled, or capable, solidifying their place at the top of the social or professional ladder.

By demeaning others, they aim to validate their sense of superiority. The methods they use to belittle others can range from overt and aggressive to subtle and insidious.

It could be a direct insult, a sarcastic remark,

or even a compliment with an underhanded edge, all intended to undermine another person's confidence.

By casting aspersions on someone's ideas, choices, or performance, especially in a public setting, they seek not only to diminish the other person's reputation but also to inflate their own.

This pattern of behavior also serves a manipulative purpose, as it alters the social dynamics to favor the Narcissist.

By reducing others, they send a message to their social group that they are the alpha, the unchallenged authority whose views and positions are paramount. They see recognition and respect as finite resources that they must hoard at the expense of others.

Furthermore, this constant belittlement is a shield for their delicate ego. Any hint of competition or display of talent from someone else is viewed as a threat, one they believe can be neutralized through ridicule or criticism.

This is often why they pinpoint individuals who are successful or admired—these are the people who represent a challenge to their self-declared supremacy.

For those who are subjected to a Narcissist's belittling, it's vital to realize that this behavior is a reflection of the Narcissist's deep-seated vulnerabilities, not the victim's deficiencies.

Keeping a robust sense of self and refusing to absorb the harmful barbs are key to maintaining one's mental and emotional health in the face of such adversity.

It's essential to remember that the problem lies with the Narcissist's insecurities and not with those they attempt to undermine.

Number Fourteen
Impersonal Connections

Narcissistic individuals often enter into connections with others that are marked by a lack of true intimacy and emotional depth.

These relationships are typically surface-level and serve primarily as a vehicle for Narcissists to enhance their own image and achieve their self-centered goals.

The fundamental essence of these interactions is transactional; the Narcissist looks to other people to supply them with the admiration and support that prop up their ego, or to assist in accomplishing their personal objectives.

Within such interactions, the Narcissist is

often the charmer, wielding their allure to ensnare those who can elevate their status or bring them benefits.

This display of interest is often contingent upon what the Narcissist can gain and typically diminishes once their needs are satisfied.

Their calculated manner of engagement is designed to garner affirmations of their worth and to satiate their hunger for acknowledgment.

Sadly, the true emotional requirements of their counterparts are frequently overlooked or dismissed in these equations.

Narcissists commonly shy away from the mutual exchange that nourishes authentic relationships.

They are more inclined to insist on the centrality of their own needs and may react with cold indifference, or even open antagonism, when others express a need for emotional sustenance or equality in the relationship.

This pattern often results in a succession of transient relationships. Should the Narcissist's goals be reached, or if their companion seeks a more emotionally equitable bond, the Narcissist might sever ties abruptly and without conscience.

In the Narcissist's world, individuals are not cherished for their inherent worth but are valued for what they can provide.

People entangled in such connections

frequently end up feeling exploited and abandoned, left with a hollow or disillusioned sentiment.

It's critical for those who find themselves in the Narcissist's sphere to recognize the self-serving dynamics at play.

Acknowledging this reality is the first step in safeguarding one's emotional health and in the pursuit of more sincere and fulfilling relationships.

Number Fifteen
Lack of Responsibility

People with Narcissistic tendencies often find it difficult to accept responsibility for their mistakes. This is a core aspect of their personality, serving to protect a self-image that is both grandiose and extremely fragile.

For them, to admit to a mistake is akin to showing a chink in their carefully constructed armor of self-perceived flawlessness.

In situations that demand a measure of accountability, such individuals are prone to shifting the blame rather than introspecting and acknowledging their role in the fault.

This behavior can be both an instinctive reflex

to defend their ego and a calculated attempt to preserve their self-assumed air of infallibility. They are adept at twisting the story, casting themselves as the unfortunate victims of external forces or the wrongdoings of others, thus diverting the focus from their own failings.

This habitual refusal to take responsibility can strain and even break personal and professional relationships. It can destroy trust and diminish respect, as those close to them may find themselves wrongly accused or held liable for the Narcissist's errors.

In a workplace, this lack of ownership can cultivate a toxic atmosphere, with coworkers or team members feeling pressured to take the fall for mistakes they did not make, fostering an environment lacking in trust and openness.

The consequences of this behavior are not just external; they impact the Narcissist's self-improvement as well. By never accepting fault, they miss out on the chance to learn and grow from their experiences.

Those who have to deal with such personalities need to be savvy to this pattern, often needing to present indisputable facts and communicate boundaries with care and assertiveness.

Nonetheless, it's important to remain prepared for a defensive response, as preserving their self-image is usually a Narcissist's utmost priority.

Number Sixteen
Impulsive Behaviors

Individuals with a strong Narcissistic streak might find themselves acting on whims and impulses, sometimes with scant regard for what might follow.

This propensity for impetuous behavior can affect not just their personal life choices but can also spill over into their professional conduct, leading to decisions that may be viewed as precipitate or even irresponsible.

These persons typically carry with them a sense of elevated privilege and a belief in their own uniqueness, which fosters a deep-seated trust in their own decision-making.

This often excessive self-belief may render them oblivious to potential dangers, as their overconfidence can obscure the need for caution. Although such confidence may appear attractive at first glance, it can be a double-edged sword, masking the real risks involved.

Driven by a craving for recognition and excitement, Narcissists might engage in spontaneous acts of daring, motivated by a desire to reinforce their persona as bold and groundbreaking.

They often hunger for the limelight and the admiration that comes with it, at times neglecting to consider the longer-range detrimental effects in favor of the immediate praise and thrill such actions garner.

For some Narcissists, impulsive behavior can act as a diversion or an antidote to feelings of dullness or psychological discomfort.

The adrenaline rush that accompanies such spur-of-the-moment conduct provides a temporary distraction and a sense of novelty. Nonetheless, this temporary high can carry significant consequences.

The repercussions of such impulsiveness can have far-reaching effects. Personal ties may be compromised when the Narcissist acts without thought for how their behavior impacts those closest to them.

Hasty financial decisions can jeopardize their economic well-being, while in the workplace, impetuous choices can result in squandered prospects or career setbacks.

Those close to individuals with these impulsive tendencies often find themselves in the unenviable position of mitigating the damage or preempting unwise decisions.

It becomes imperative to create clear boundaries and to articulate the potential impacts of hasty actions clearly.

Yet, in making these interventions, there's an understanding that such guidance may go unheeded, given the Narcissist's preoccupation with their immediate wants and the maintenance of their self-image.

Number Seventeen
Charming but Insincere

People with a Narcissistic streak are often the life of the party, exuding a magnetism that draws others in.

Their charm, however, isn't a natural extension of a warm personality; it's a strategic act designed to influence and win over those around them.

This charm is deployed with precision, tailored to what the Narcissist perceives others want to see or hear, all to fulfill their personal ambitions or needs.

Yet, this beguiling veneer masks an authentic absence of depth in their interactions. The

Narcissist's engagements are not anchored in a true connection with others but are instead exercises in achieving their own ends.

They view their relationships as transactions, with people being of interest only so long as they serve a purpose for the Narcissist.

This superficial charm is often fleeting, only sustained as long as it serves their interests. When their goals are met or if individuals are no longer of use to them, the Narcissist's enthusiasm and warmth can evaporate, leaving a cold indifference in its wake.

Those who once felt valued by the Narcissist might soon find themselves feeling discarded, realizing too late that the initial affection was merely a ploy.

The stark contrast between the Narcissist's captivating front and their genuine lack of concern becomes starkly clear when their needs are met.

What was once warmth and interest can turn into disinterest or even disdain. This abrupt change can be jarring and painful for those who mistook the Narcissist's charm for real interest or kinship.

It's essential for anyone dealing with a Narcissist to understand this dynamic. Recognizing that their charm often has an ulterior motive can help maintain emotional caution and emphasize the need for personal boundaries to safeguard one's emotional health and self-respect.

Number Eighteen
Difficulty with Boundaries

People who exhibit Narcissistic traits often seem to have a blind spot when it comes to respecting the boundaries of those around them.

Their self-focused nature can overshadow the usual sensitivity to social cues and personal limits that dictate how most individuals interact. Consequently, they might unwittingly cross lines that are implicitly understood and usually unbroken, such as personal space or the flow of a conversation.

Narcissists may, without ill intent, dominate discussions, derailing them to highlight their own opinions or achievements, oblivious to the social faux pas they are committing.

They might probe into personal matters without hesitation or give advice no one asked for, presuming their perspectives are always warranted and welcomed.

Physically, they might not recognize the concept of personal space, standing too close or initiating contact that others might find intrusive.

Their sense of entitlement may lead them to handle or claim others' property without prior consent, or they might assume an unwarranted role in others' activities and decisions.

When confronted about such intrusions, Narcissists are often taken aback, not necessarily out of malice, but from a genuine lack of understanding that their actions are out of bounds.

This could stem from their belief in their own exceptionalism, a belief that exempts them from the norms that govern everyone else's social conduct.

The ripple effects of their disregard for boundaries can strain or even sever relationships.

Those on the receiving end may experience a range of negative emotions, from mild irritation to deep-seated anger and distrust, which might prompt them to withdraw from the Narcissist to safeguard their sense of autonomy and respect.

Navigating this aspect of a Narcissist's behavior demands direct and transparent communication. Asserting firm boundaries and reinforcing them consistently can guide the Narcissist toward more acceptable social interactions.

Nevertheless, those dealing with Narcissists must brace for resistance and remain resolute in upholding their established limits, since Narcissists typically challenge any restriction that impedes their self-serving behavior.

Number Nineteen
Projection

Projection, a term rooted in psychology, refers to the act of attributing one's own undesirable thoughts or behaviors onto someone else.

This can be a common trait among those with Narcissistic tendencies, where they deflect their own shortcomings by attributing them to others.

By doing so, they not only reject any personal fault but also inflict the discomfort of those shortcomings onto someone else.

Narcissists often use projection as a shield for their ego; they craft an image of themselves that is without flaw and when their behavior doesn't align with this ideal, they project that behavior onto others.

This allows them to maintain a self-concept that is unmarred by the less savory aspects of their personality or actions.

Moreover, projection works as a tactic to divert attention away from themselves. If a Narcissist is confronted with a mistake or a misbehavior, they may project that very issue onto the person holding them accountable.

For instance, if they are accused of being manipulative, they might counter by accusing the other person of the same behavior.

This kind of psychological maneuvering can lead to a distorted view of reality for those around the Narcissist.

Being wrongly accused of the Narcissist's own behaviors can cause confusion and emotional turmoil. The affected individuals may begin to doubt their own actions and thoughts, leading to a state of self-questioning that stems from the Narcissist's deceptive assertions.

Recognizing the mechanism of projection is important in dealing with Narcissists. Understanding that their accusations might actually be confessions in disguise can be liberating and protective for those who would otherwise be mired in the Narcissist's manipulative tactics.

Keeping an emotional distance and establishing firm personal boundaries can help maintain one's sense of reality and emotional

integrity when faced with such challenging
interactions.

Number Twenty
Gaslighting

In the complex dance of human interaction, the manipulation tactic known as gaslighting is akin to a psychological shadow play.

It's a deliberate strategy where one person aims to dim the lights on another's sense of reality, memory, and sanity, ever so gradually.

Those who display Narcissistic traits may resort to this approach as a means to tighten their grip of influence over someone else's mind.

Within the tangled web of gaslighting, the Narcissist will carefully choreograph each move to cast doubt on the victim's beliefs and feelings.

They may spin a web of lies, boldly deny clear facts, or label genuine emotional responses as overblown or entirely misplaced. Their ultimate goal is not just to question but to uproot the victim's own trust in their perceptions and convictions.

Consider a scenario where an individual brings up an issue to a Narcissist, perhaps calling out a problematic action.

The Narcissist, in a classic gaslighting maneuver, might outright dismiss the occurrence, warp the memory of the event, or paint the individual as overly sensitive or utterly confused.

This isn't just a defense—it's an offensive

strategy that places the victim in a mental maze, constantly second-guessing their sanity and truth.

What makes gaslighting so devastating is its ability to chip away at the foundation of a person's self-identity and worth. It fosters a toxic dependence, wherein the victim may start to rely on the very person distorting their reality, further solidifying the Narcissist's hold over them.

Breaking free from the gaslighting cycle demands a keen eye and unwavering resolve. Those ensnared by such tactics must learn to recognize the signs and hold fast to their own experiences, reinforcing them with the concrete evidence of records and recollections.

It often necessitates the support of allies grounded in truth and, sometimes, a strategic retreat from the Narcissist's sphere of influence to halt the erosion of one's sense of self.

It's a journey back to trusting one's inner compass, reclaiming autonomy in the narrative of one's life.

My Testimony

My journey out of the clutches of a Love-Bombing Narcissist called Maverick imparted a crucial lesson: escape transcends physical separation; it's fundamentally about emotional and psychological freedom.

Over 28 years ago, I started penning the chapters of my life, chronicling the trials and tribulations of my experience. That manuscript, filled with raw emotion and unfiltered truth, found itself relegated to the confinement of a closet, locked away for numerous reasons.

The most potent of these was shame. Back then, my knowledge of narcissism and Love

Bombing was nonexistent; I mistook my naivety for foolishness, branding myself as gullible.

Revisiting the most harrowing chapters of my life posed an immense challenge. To understand how I could have been so susceptible to someone like Maverick, I had to peel back the layers of my upbringing, to unearth the potential origins of my vulnerability.

Time propelled me forward, and after more than a quarter of a century, I mustered the courage to confront my past. Retrieving the dusty manuscripts, I embarked on a mission to refine them, preparing my story for the world.

Under the pseudonym Alexandria O'Neal, I titled my memoir series "Hallways of Her Past."

The transformative moment came in 2023, while revising my books. My friend Allison, who often shares enlightening video snippets with me, sent me a clip that introduced the concept of 'Love Bombing.' It was a revelation. I was familiar with the term 'Narcissist,' and while Maverick fit that description, it didn't completely encapsulate his manipulative tactics. The missing piece was 'Love Bombing,' a strategy he had mastered.

Acknowledging this didn't just give me clarity—it provided peace. For years, I had been tormented by the insidious belief that I was fabricating the dysfunction in my head, a belief Maverick had instilled in me. The realization that I wasn't insane was a monumental release.

My intention in sharing my memoir isn't solely to encourage readership, though I do hope my words reach those who need them.

More than anything, it's about offering support and possibly preventing others from enduring similar ordeals. Through my real-life narratives, I lay bare the step-by-step progression of genuine Love Bombing mixed with narcissism.

If my experiences resonate with you or could illuminate your path, then I invite you to delve into my series "Hallways of Her Past." May my past serve as a beacon, guiding you away from the shadows cast by Love Bombing Narcissists, like Maverick.

Addiction and Bad Behavior

Dopamine, a crucial neurotransmitter, functions as a messenger within the brain and body, playing a pivotal role in how we experience motivation and pleasure.

Let's delve into how indulgences like chocolate and coffee engage with this system to influence our feelings and behavior.

The allure of chocolate can be traced back to its rich tapestry of compounds, with one in particular, phenylethylamine, standing out.

This compound has the ability to trigger a cascade of feel-good chemicals, including endorphins, and notably, it elevates dopamine levels, which can lift one's mood and foster a sense of contentment.

The indulgence in dark chocolate is especially impactful due to its higher cocoa content, rich in flavanols believed to enhance cerebral blood flow, and thereby, dopamine release. Moreover, the creamy fats found in chocolate slow the digestive process, prolonging these delightful sensations.

Shifting to coffee, its claim to fame is the caffeine it harbors—a potent force that sharpens our mental alertness. Caffeine's magic lies in its ability to block adenosine, a neurotransmitter that typically encourages sleep and reduces stimulation, thus allowing dopamine to surge and keep us more awake and focused.

But when the joy of our guilty pleasures becomes a routine, our brains may recalibrate, affecting the natural balance of neurotransmitters and their sensitivity.

If we abruptly stop the intake of chocolate or coffee, our system might need time to find its equilibrium, which can result in withdrawal symptoms. For chocolate, these are often mild—think cravings or a headache—stemming from a psychological need rather than a physical one.

Caffeine's grip, however, is stronger. Ceasing its consumption can lead to more intense withdrawal symptoms including persistent headaches, fatigue, and a noticeable dip in energy and alertness.

Some might find themselves feeling unusually

irritable or unable to concentrate, and these symptoms can linger anywhere from a couple of days to over a week, influenced by how much caffeine was a regular part of your diet and personal sensitivity.

Chocolate and coffee do more than just tickle the palate; they enhance our dopamine levels, making us feel good. Yet, it's this very sensation that, when absent, can cause our bodies to exhibit withdrawal symptoms, with coffee generally presenting a more challenging rebound due to its higher caffeine levels.

The relationship with a Love Bombing Narcissist can indeed be likened to a cyclical addiction to substances like chocolate or caffeine, where the highs are euphoric and the lows are painfully stark.

At the core of this dynamic is the interplay of anticipation and reward—a pattern deeply etched into our psychology and neural pathways.

When a Narcissist showers you with affection and attention, it's as if you're indulging in the richest chocolate, or sipping the most aromatic coffee. Your brain lights up, dopamine floods your system, and you feel a surge of pleasure, a rewarding high that signals everything is right in the world.

This Love Bombing phase is the sweet spot, the caffeine kick, that first irresistible layer of flavor that captures your senses completely.

But as the pattern unfolds, the Love Bomber

often withdraws the very attention and affection that triggered your dopamine response.

Suddenly, you're left in an emotional withdrawal akin to the slump after a sugar crash or the headache from a lack of caffeine.

There's a yearning, a deep craving for more of those intense moments of sweetness and stimulation. Just as the body can crave the alertness that caffeine brings, your psyche craves the validation and intense connection that the Narcissist initially provided.

Then, in a twist of events, the Love Bomber returns with soothing affection, mirroring the comfort of a warm, familiar mug of cocoa on a cold day or that invigorating sip of coffee that breaks through the fog.

The cycle repeats, each phase of abuse followed by reconciliation acting as a hit, reactivating the centers of your brain that have learned this routine and have become habituated to this tumultuous rhythm of highs and lows.

Being in such a relationship, you become conditioned to the pattern—abuse followed by soothing, much like the addictive pattern of indulgence followed by the inevitable crash, then craving more.

Your mental state becomes tied to this cycle, leaving you in a precarious balance that hinges on the whims of another, much as your energy might pendulate with your next caffeine fix.

The psychological hooks of a Love Bombing Narcissist are potent and difficult to untangle from, not unlike the grasp of our favorite vices on our wellbeing.

Recognizing this pattern is akin to understanding our own susceptibilities to cravings and addictions—both are critical first steps towards seeking a healthier equilibrium.

Kinda Narcissistic?

It's not unusual for people to occasionally exhibit characteristics that could be labeled as narcissistic. The key is understanding that this doesn't immediately point to Narcissistic Personality Disorder (NPD).

We all sit somewhere on the spectrum of narcissism, which stretches from the occasional self-centered moment right up to the more serious, clinical end of the scale, where a mental health diagnosis might come into play. From time to time, we all might:

-Look for validation or praise from those around us.

-Speak highly of our own achievements,

perhaps stretching the truth a little.

-Consider ourselves to have unique attributes or talents.

-Daydream about achieving great things or attracting admirers.

-Feel a sting of jealousy or assume others might envy what we have.

These behaviors are part and parcel of the human condition. In fact, a dash of this self-regard can actually be beneficial, driving us to strive for more, take the helm in group situations, or simply hold our heads high with self-assurance.

The red flags start waving, however, when these tendencies become excessive and start to interfere with our day-to-day lives or our interpersonal relationships. That's when they might be symptomatic of NPD.

In contrast to someone with full-blown narcissism, individuals who just have a few such traits will often still:

-Demonstrate real empathy and care for others' feelings and well-being.

-Cultivate and cherish deep, meaningful relationships.

-Show a capacity for introspection and a willingness to change when their actions aren't appropriate.

-Feel genuinely sorry if their actions have been hurtful or self-centered.

It's worth noting that narcissistic behavior isn't static; it can wax and wane with life's phases. For example, the teenage years are often marked by a heightened sense of self-importance, but this usually mellows with maturity.

Recognizing the gray areas in personality traits is vital. Most of us are complex blends of characteristics that can be beneficial or problematic, depending on the context and how they manifest.

For anyone uneasy about their personality traits and the impact they might be having, professional advice can be invaluable.

Psychologists and therapists are equipped to help unravel these complex threads, offering strategies to cope with, or adjust, aspects of our behavior that we might find troubling.

GET OUT!

Embarking on the journey to liberate yourself from the grip of a Narcissist is akin to stepping out from an eclipse into the sun; it's the beginning of a new chapter that is entirely yours to write.

This chapter of your journey will be penned with courage, will be underscored by meticulous care, and will be defined by a resilience that endures even when the road seems unyielding and protracted.

It's not merely a few steps away; it is a continuous march toward the essence of your own freedom. In the delicate dance of distancing yourself from such toxicity, your safety and well-being are the non-negotiable partners.

They are the constants in an equation that may at times feel unsolvable. The process is not instantaneous, and unforeseen turns may appear, adding complexity to your course.

Yet, with each considered move, remember that you are charting a course to a place where your peace of mind is the very air you breathe.

In the thick of change, the touchstone of support is invaluable. Be it the comforting embrace of loved ones, the compassionate ear of friends, or the guiding voice of counselors, their collective presence is a fortress of solidarity.

They will share the burden, echo your resolve, and stand as pillars when fatigue beckons. Seeking support is not a sign of weakness but an embrace of collective strength.

In those quiet moments of introspection, where doubt may whisper with a hiss, hold fast to an unwavering truth: You are inherently deserving of a life unmarred by manipulation, a life where your happiness is not just an option but the very foundation.

This seismic shift you're contemplating? It's crafted by you, for you, and starts the very moment you choose it.

With each conscious act of self-kindness, you're staging a silent revolution against the oppressive shadow of narcissism. These acts are the lifeblood of your newfound strength, nourishing your spirit into not just enduring but flourishing.

Severing the ties with a Narcissist is nothing short of an odyssey toward hope—a signal to the universe and yourself that brighter days are not just imagined but achievable. It's a testament to the unshakable self-respect you're cultivating and the pure, unfettered love you're allowing yourself to embrace.

Navigate this path with mindful steps, with the wisdom of protection, but above all, with the unwavering conviction in your heart that the freedom on the horizon is yours for the taking.

WARNING

Throughout the earlier sections of this book, I've woven in some playful nomenclature to highlight the deceitful traits that some individuals possess, all in an effort to make these situations feel familiar and accessible.

However, at this juncture, I feel it's crucial to double back and address the seriousness of disentangling oneself from the clutches of a Love Bomber. It cannot be stressed enough that seeking the expertise of a qualified professional is essential when planning your exit.

This text is crafted to cast light on the hallmarks of Love Bombing and to offer guidance on forging a path to freedom.

Nevertheless, it's vitally important to understand that a truly safe escape often hinges on specialized knowledge and assistance. Your safety is the priority, and enlisting professional help to devise and execute an escape plan is not just advisable; it's imperative for your protection.

Please check out all the books in this series:

Hallways of Her Past-A Damaged Soul

Hallways of Her Past-A Twisted Soul

Hallways of Her Past-An Afflicted Soul

Hallways of Her Past-An Innocent Soul

Hallways of Her Past-A Timid Soul

Hallways of Her Past-A Renewed Soul-Coming Soon

Hallways of Her Past-A Redeemed Soul-Coming Soon

20 Tell-Tale Signs You're With a Love Scammer-Coming Soon

If you like my books, please leave an honest review on Amazon, Goodreads, or other book-lover sites. Reviews are helpful for authors, especially like me, who are independently published. They help make other people aware that my books are out there.